How to Become
a Real Rainmaker

Content

Introduction

What is a Rainmaker and why it's a crucial role for businesses.

In the dynamic world of business, a Rainmaker is an individual with a unique set of skills and attributes, capable of generating an abundance of revenue and driving substantial growth for their organization. Just as the name suggests, a Rainmaker possesses the ability to bring forth a torrential downpour of success, turning prospects into loyal clients and deals into long-term partnerships. This role goes beyond mere salesmanship; it's about cultivating and nurturing relationships, foreseeing opportunities, and having the foresight to harness them effectively. In essence, a Rainmaker is the driving force behind a company's prosperity, making this role absolutely crucial for businesses seeking sustainable success in a competitive landscape.

One of the fundamental aspects that distinguish a Rainmaker from an average salesperson is their mastery of the product or service they represent. They go beyond surface-level knowledge and dive deep into the intricacies of what they offer. This expertise not only instills confidence in potential clients but also allows Rainmakers to tailor their pitch to meet the specific needs and pain points of each customer. Consequently, clients feel understood and valued, fostering a higher likelihood of conversion.

Furthermore, Rainmakers excel in the art of building and expanding their network of contacts. They actively seek out networking opportunities, attend industry events, and leverage online platforms to connect with professionals and potential clients. By cultivating a strong network, Rainmakers create a robust support system that propels them to uncover new business opportunities and expand their sphere of influence.

A key attribute that sets Rainmakers apart is their exceptional communication skills. They possess the ability to captivate an audience, whether in person or through written communication.

Through persuasive and engaging presentations, Rainmakers can effectively convey the value of their offerings and establish an emotional connection with prospects. This skill proves instrumental in building lasting relationships and securing long-term partnerships.

Identifying and understanding the target market is another crucial aspect that Rainmakers meticulously address. By conducting thorough market research, they gain insights into the pain points, preferences, and needs of potential clients. Armed with this knowledge, Rainmakers can customize their approach and present solutions that directly address the challenges faced by their target audience. This tailored approach significantly enhances the likelihood of closing deals successfully.

Rainmakers also focus on the long game by building genuine and meaningful relationships with their clients. Rather than viewing sales as a one-time transaction, they understand that fostering trust and rapport leads to customer loyalty and repeat business. By providing exceptional customer service, going above and beyond expectations, and consistently delivering value, Rainmakers earn a reputation that encourages referrals and word-of-mouth marketing.

In the realm of Rainmakers, setting clear and measurable goals is of paramount importance. They establish ambitious yet achievable targets for revenue generation, client acquisition, and market penetration. These goals serve as guiding beacons, keeping Rainmakers motivated and focused on the tasks at hand. Regularly monitoring their progress, they adapt their strategies to navigate challenges and seize emerging opportunities.

However, the path to becoming a Rainmaker is not without obstacles. Rejections and setbacks are inevitable in the world of sales. What sets a Rainmaker apart is their persistence and resilience in the face of adversity. They view challenges as opportunities for growth and learning, using each experience to refine their approach and hone their skills.

To be a Rainmaker is to be a perpetual student of the craft. Continuous learning and self-improvement are woven into the fabric of their success. Rainmakers stay updated on industry trends, new technologies, and sales techniques. They attend workshops, seminars, and courses, constantly seeking ways to enhance their abilities and remain ahead of the curve.

The role of a Rainmaker is pivotal in the realm of business success. These individuals possess a potent combination of product mastery, exceptional communication skills, relationship-building prowess, and an unyielding drive to excel. By understanding their target market, setting clear goals, and persevering in the face of challenges, Rainmakers become the catalysts of success for their organizations, creating a positive impact that resonates far beyond mere monetary gains. They shape the course of their business, and in doing so, become the architects of their own prosperous destiny.

The importance of becoming a Rainmaker and how it can influence one's career and professional success.

Becoming a Rainmaker can be a transformative journey that significantly influences one's career and professional success. The importance of adopting the Rainmaker mindset and honing the associated skills goes beyond simply driving revenue for an organization; it can be a game-changer on multiple levels.

First and foremost, being a Rainmaker allows individuals to stand out in their respective industries. In a competitive business landscape, where numerous professionals are vying for attention and opportunities, the ability to consistently generate substantial revenue and bring in new clients sets Rainmakers apart. This recognition and reputation as a top performer can open doors to new career prospects, promotions, and leadership roles.

A Rainmaker's impact on their organization goes beyond immediate financial gains. Their ability to cultivate strong client relationships and deliver exceptional customer service fosters loyalty among existing clients. This, in turn, leads to repeat business, referrals, and positive word-of-mouth, creating a steady stream of ongoing revenue for the company. The trust and credibility they build with clients also solidify the organization's reputation and position it as a go-to provider in the market.

The Rainmaker's influence on team dynamics is equally significant. Their determination, passion, and success-driven attitude can be contagious, inspiring colleagues and fostering a high-performance culture within the organization. As Rainmakers share their knowledge and mentor others, they contribute to the overall growth and development of the team, further elevating the company's potential for success.

Beyond immediate job-related benefits, adopting the Rainmaker mindset can have a profound impact on personal and professional growth. Developing the necessary skills to excel as a Rainmaker, such as communication, networking, and negotiation abilities, can be applied to various aspects of life, both inside and outside the workplace. The confidence gained through successful client interactions and deal-closing experiences can spill over into other areas, leading to increased self-assurance and assertiveness.

Moreover, the pursuit of Rainmaker status drives continuous improvement and lifelong learning. Rainmakers are constantly on the lookout for innovative solutions, emerging trends, and new techniques that can elevate their performance further. This quest for knowledge and self-improvement fuels personal growth and keeps Rainmakers at the forefront of their field.

From a financial standpoint, the impact of being a Rainmaker is substantial. The ability to consistently bring in new business and secure lucrative deals often results in higher earning potential. As Rainmakers contribute significantly to a company's revenue, they are likely to be recognized and rewarded with attractive compensation packages, performance bonuses, and commission-based incentives.

Beyond immediate financial gains, the Rainmaker status can enhance career stability and longevity. Businesses highly value individuals who can consistently generate revenue, making Rainmakers less susceptible to downsizing and economic downturns. In times of uncertainty, their skills become even more critical to an organization's survival and growth, cementing their position as invaluable assets.

In conclusion, becoming a Rainmaker is not just about driving revenue; it is a transformative journey that positively impacts one's career and professional success. From elevating one's reputation and standing out in the industry to fostering team growth and personal development, Rainmakers have the potential to shape their careers and influence their organization's trajectory. The pursuit of Rainmaker status is a continuous and rewarding endeavor that can lead to financial prosperity, personal fulfillment, and lasting success in the ever-evolving world of business.

Master Your Product or Service

Dive into how to become an expert in the product or service you are selling.

Becoming an expert in the product or service you are selling is an essential aspect of becoming a Rainmaker. Clients seek confidence and trust in those they do business with, and being an authority on what you offer not only instills that trust but also helps you tailor your pitch to meet their specific needs. Here's how you can become an expert in your product or service:

Understanding the Features and Benefits:

Start by immersing yourself in the details of what you're selling. Study the features, specifications, and functionalities of your product or service. Understand how it stands out from competitors and the unique benefits it offers to clients. This knowledge will serve as the foundation for your sales pitch and enable you to communicate the value proposition effectively.

Leveraging Internal Resources:

Tap into the expertise of your colleagues, product managers, and subject matter experts within your organization. Engage in discussions with them to gain deeper insights into the product or service and its applications. Understanding the intricacies from different perspectives will equip you with a comprehensive understanding.

Staying Updated on Product Developments:

Products and services evolve over time, with updates and enhancements being introduced regularly. Stay current with these developments by attending product training sessions, webinars, and reading relevant documentation. Being up-to-date ensures that you provide accurate and timely information to potential clients.

Learning from Customer Feedback:

Customer feedback is an invaluable resource for refining your understanding of the product or service. Listen to what customers are saying about their experiences, pain points, and expectations. Take note of any recurring themes or suggestions for improvement. By addressing customer concerns, you demonstrate that you are invested in providing the best solution for their needs.

Engaging in Hands-on Experience:

Whenever possible, gain hands-on experience with the product or service. If you're selling software, explore its functionalities and features by using it yourself. For tangible products, handle them, understand how they work, and explore various use cases. Direct experience will deepen your knowledge and enhance your ability to demonstrate the product or service's value.

Researching the Market and Competitors:

Study the market landscape and analyze your competitors' offerings. Understanding what sets your product or service apart from others in the market will help you articulate its unique selling points. Identify your key differentiators and use them to position your offerings as the ideal solution for your clients.

Attending Industry Events and Webinars:

Participate in industry events, trade shows, and webinars related to your product or service. These platforms offer opportunities to learn from industry experts, gain insights into market trends, and expand your network. Networking with like-minded professionals can provide valuable perspectives and ideas.

Creating Educational Content:

Teach others about your product or service by creating educational content. Write blog posts, record video tutorials, or deliver presentations about various aspects of the offering. Educating others not only solidifies your expertise but also positions you as a valuable resource for potential clients.

Seeking Certification and Training:

If applicable, seek certifications or specialized training related to your product or service. Industry-recognized certifications add credibility to your expertise and demonstrate your commitment to continuous learning.

Practicing and Refining Your Pitch:

Finally, practice articulating the features, benefits, and use cases of your product or service. Practice with colleagues or friends and seek feedback on your delivery. Refining your pitch through practice will boost your confidence and make you more effective in communicating with potential clients.

Becoming an expert in your product or service is an ongoing process. The more you invest in learning and understanding, the better equipped you'll be to position yourself as a knowledgeable and trustworthy Rainmaker, ready to provide valuable solutions to your clients.

Provide tips on learning the features and benefits of the product to effectively communicate them to potential clients.

Effectively learning and communicating the features and benefits of a product to potential clients is a crucial skill for becoming a Rainmaker. Here are some tips to help you master this aspect of sales:

Thoroughly Study the Product

Immerse yourself in the product by thoroughly studying its features, specifications, and functionalities. Take the time to understand how it works, what problems it solves, and the value it brings to customers. The more you know about the product, the more confidently you can communicate its benefits.

Use the Product Yourself

Whenever possible, use the product yourself. Hands-on experience will give you a deeper understanding of its capabilities and limitations. This personal experience will also allow you to share real-life examples and anecdotes with potential clients, making your communication more relatable and authentic.

Focus on Customer Benefits

While knowing the technical details is essential, remember that clients are more interested in the benefits the product provides than its features. Shift your focus from technical jargon to the tangible benefits it offers to customers. Understand how the product addresses specific pain points and meets the needs of your target market.

Listen to Customer Feedback

Pay close attention to feedback from existing customers. Understand their experiences, challenges, and the positive outcomes they achieved using the product. This firsthand information will help you shape your communication to address the concerns and interests of potential clients.

Tailor Your Pitch to the Client's Needs

Avoid a one-size-fits-all approach and customize your communication for each potential client. Before the meeting, research their specific needs and pain points. During the conversation, emphasize how the product's features directly address their unique challenges. Demonstrating that you understand their specific requirements will make your pitch more compelling.

Practice Active Listening

During meetings with potential clients, practice active listening. Pay attention to their questions, concerns, and reactions. This will enable you to identify which product features are most relevant to their needs. Tailor your communication based on the feedback you receive to ensure a more engaging and personalized presentation.

Use Analogies and Stories

Complex product features can sometimes be challenging for clients to grasp immediately. Use analogies and stories to illustrate how the product works and the benefits it offers. Analogies can simplify technical concepts and make them more accessible to non-technical clients.

Showcase Case Studies and Success Stories

Share case studies and success stories of how the product has made a positive impact on other clients. Real-life examples demonstrate the practical applications and results the product can achieve, reinforcing its value proposition.

Provide Demonstrations and Visuals

Whenever possible, provide live demonstrations of the product's features. Visual aids, such as charts, infographics, and product videos, can enhance your communication and make it more memorable for potential clients.

Seek Continuous Feedback

Regularly seek feedback from your sales team, colleagues, or managers on your communication style and effectiveness. Continuous improvement is essential in refining your pitch and increasing your success as a Rainmaker.

Build a Strong Network of Contacts

Effective networking strategies to expand the circle of contacts.

Effective networking is a powerful tool for Rainmakers to expand their circle of contacts, build meaningful relationships, and uncover new business opportunities. Approach networking with authenticity and a genuine interest in getting to know others. People appreciate sincerity, and building connections based on trust and mutual respect lays a strong foundation for fruitful relationships. Avoid solely focusing on self-promotion; instead, seek to understand the needs and interests of others and find ways to offer value.

Take advantage of industry events and conferences as they provide excellent opportunities to meet like-minded professionals, potential clients, and industry influencers. Be proactive in attending relevant gatherings, seminars, and workshops. Engage in conversations, exchange business cards, and follow up with individuals afterward to solidify the connections made.

In today's digital age, online networking platforms, especially LinkedIn, are essential for expanding one's professional network. Maintain an up-to-date and engaging profile that showcases your expertise and accomplishments. Actively participate in relevant groups, join discussions, and connect with professionals who share similar interests or work in related fields.

Hosting or participating in webinars and workshops on topics related to your expertise can attract professionals interested in your area of specialization. Such events position you as a thought leader and provide an opportunity to engage with potential clients and collaborators. Collect contact information from attendees and follow up afterward to nurture the connections.

Participating in community and charity events not only allows you to give back but also provides networking opportunities. Engaging in activities aligned with your values and interests can lead to meeting like-minded individuals who may become valuable contacts in the future.

Don't hesitate to ask your existing contacts for referrals or introductions to individuals who may benefit from your product or services. Personal recommendations carry significant weight and can open doors to new opportunities.

After meeting new contacts, always follow up promptly. Send a personalized message or email to express appreciation for the interaction and express interest in staying connected. Regularly keep in touch with your network by sharing relevant content, congratulating them on their achievements, or offering support when needed.

Become a connector by introducing individuals within your network who could benefit from knowing each other. This act of generosity strengthens your relationships and positions you as a valuable resource within your network.

While social media is a powerful networking tool, use it responsibly and professionally. Avoid controversial topics and be mindful of what you share publicly. Present yourself in a manner that aligns with your personal brand and professional objectives.

Get involved in local business communities and Chamber of Commerce events. These gatherings often bring together professionals from various industries, providing an excellent platform to establish connections with potential clients and collaborators in your area.

By adopting these effective networking strategies, Rainmakers can steadily expand their circle of contacts, strengthen relationships, and create a robust network that opens doors to new opportunities and contributes to long-term business success.

15 Advices on maintaining and nurturing professional relationships in the long term.

Maintaining and nurturing professional relationships in the long term is essential for Rainmakers to sustain success and cultivate a strong network of valuable contacts. Here are some pieces of advice to help you excel in this aspect:

1. Stay in Regular Contact: Regularly reach out to your contacts to check in, share updates, or congratulate them on their achievements. Keeping the lines of communication open demonstrates that you value the relationship and are genuinely interested in their well-being.

2. Personalize Your Interactions: Tailor your communications to each individual, acknowledging their specific interests and needs. Avoid generic or automated messages, as they can come across as insincere. Personal touches show that you value the person and the relationship.

3. Remember Important Dates: Make an effort to remember important dates such as birthdays, work anniversaries, or significant milestones. Sending personalized messages or small tokens of appreciation can go a long way in strengthening your connections.

4. Offer Support and Assistance: Be proactive in offering your support and assistance when your contacts need help. Whether it's providing guidance, making introductions, or sharing valuable resources, being a reliable and supportive resource fosters trust and goodwill.

5. Be a Good Listener: When engaging with your contacts, be an attentive listener. Pay attention to their concerns, aspirations, and challenges. Showing genuine interest in their experiences and perspectives strengthens the bond and demonstrates empathy.

6. Seek Opportunities to Collaborate: Look for ways to collaborate with your contacts on projects, events, or initiatives. Working together on shared goals can deepen the relationship and create mutual benefits.

7. Express Gratitude: Take the time to express gratitude to your contacts for their support, advice, or contributions. A simple thank-you note or email can leave a lasting positive impression.

8. Stay Updated on Their Careers: Keep track of your contacts' professional journeys. Celebrate their accomplishments and be supportive during times of transition or career advancements.

9. Attend Networking Events Together: Whenever possible, attend networking events, conferences, or workshops together with your contacts. Shared experiences in professional settings can strengthen the bond and provide opportunities for collaboration.

10. Be Honest and Transparent: In your interactions, always be honest and transparent. Building trust is a foundational element of long-term relationships, and being open about your intentions and expectations is crucial.

11. Respect Their Time: Respect your contacts' time and commitments. Be mindful of their schedules when requesting meetings or follow-ups. Being considerate of their time shows professionalism and respect.

12. Stay Positive and Positive: Maintain a positive and upbeat demeanor in your interactions. Positivity is contagious and leaves a lasting impression on others.

13. Celebrate Milestones Together: Acknowledge significant milestones in each other's careers and lives. Celebrating successes together fosters a sense of camaraderie and mutual support.

14. Be Patient and Understanding: Professional relationships, like any other, may experience ups and downs. Be patient and understanding during challenging times, and be willing to work through any obstacles that may arise.

15. Follow Through on Promises: If you make commitments or promises to your contacts, follow through on them. Reliability and

accountability are crucial in maintaining trust.

By following these pieces of advice, Rainmakers can establish and nurture strong professional relationships that contribute to their long-term success and create a supportive and robust network of contacts. Remember, investing time and effort in maintaining relationships can lead to a wealth of opportunities and enriching experiences throughout your career journey.

Develop Exceptional Communication Skills

Tips for improving both verbal and written communication skills.

Improving both verbal and written communication skills is vital for Rainmakers to effectively convey their ideas, build rapport, and influence others. Here are some tips to enhance these essential communication abilities:

Verbal Communication Skills:

1. Practice Active Listening: Focus on listening attentively to others during conversations. Avoid interrupting and genuinely try to understand their perspective before responding. Active listening enhances understanding and fosters better communication.

2. Be Clear and Concise: Express your ideas in a clear and straightforward manner. Avoid using jargon or overly complex language that might confuse your audience. Get to the point while providing sufficient context for clarity.

3. Maintain Eye Contact: When engaging in face-to-face conversations, maintain appropriate eye contact. It conveys sincerity, confidence, and interest in the discussion.

4. Adapt to Your Audience: Tailor your communication style to suit the needs and preferences of your audience. Use language and examples that resonate with them and align with their level of expertise.

5. Use Positive Body Language: Project confidence and openness through positive body language. Stand or sit upright, use appropriate hand gestures, and smile when appropriate. A positive demeanor enhances the impact of your message.

6. Practice Public Speaking: Engage in public speaking opportunities to build confidence and improve your verbal communication skills.

Join public speaking clubs like Toastmasters or practice in front of supportive friends or colleagues.

7. Seek Feedback: Request feedback from trusted peers or mentors on your verbal communication. Constructive criticism can help identify areas for improvement and refine your delivery.

Written Communication Skills:

1. Organize Your Thoughts: Before writing, outline the main points you want to convey. Organize your thoughts logically to ensure a coherent and structured message.

2. Use Plain Language: Write in a clear, straightforward manner. Avoid excessive jargon, and use language that is easily understandable by your target audience.

3. Proofread and Edit: Always proofread your writing for errors in grammar, punctuation, and spelling. Edit your work to ensure clarity and precision in your message.

4. Be Mindful of Tone: Consider the tone of your writing and how it may be perceived by the reader. Aim for a professional and courteous tone in business communications.

5. Keep it Concise: Be concise in your writing to respect the reader's time and attention. Avoid unnecessary wordiness and get to the point quickly.

6. Know Your Audience: Understand the needs and expectations of your audience before writing. Tailor your message to their interests and requirements.

7. Use Visual Aids: Incorporate relevant visuals, such as charts, graphs, or images, to enhance your written communication and make complex information more accessible.

8. Read Regularly: Reading a diverse range of materials can improve your vocabulary, writing style, and overall communication skills.

9. Seek Writing Feedback: Ask for feedback from colleagues or mentors on your written work. Constructive feedback can help you identify areas for improvement and enhance your writing.

10. Practice Regularly: Like any skill, practice is essential for improving written communication. Write regularly, such as maintaining a journal or starting a blog, to refine your writing abilities.

Some examples of successful presentations and pitches.

Certainly! Here are some examples of successful presentations and pitches that have made a significant impact:

1 . The TED Talk: "Do Schools Kill Creativity?" by Sir Ken Robinson:

In this iconic TED Talk, Sir Ken Robinson delivers a captivating presentation on the importance of nurturing creativity in education. With a perfect blend of humor, storytelling, and thought-provoking insights, Robinson challenges conventional views on education and captures the audience's attention from start to finish.

2. Apple's iPhone Launch Presentation by Steve Jobs:

Steve Jobs was renowned for his exceptional presentation skills, and one of his most memorable pitches was the unveiling of the first iPhone in 2007. Jobs masterfully showcased the revolutionary features of the iPhone, building anticipation and excitement among the audience. His passion and showmanship turned the launch event into a historic moment in the tech industry.

3. Elon Musk's Tesla Powerwall Presentation:

Elon Musk is known for his ability to captivate audiences during his presentations. In one such event, he introduced Tesla's Powerwall, a home battery storage product. Musk's clear communication, use of visuals, and compelling vision for sustainable energy solutions left a lasting impact on the audience and generated widespread interest in the product.

4. <u>Simon Sinek's "Start with Why" Presentation:</u>

Simon Sinek's TED Talk, "How Great Leaders Inspire Action," has become one of the most-watched TED Talks of all time. Sinek uses the golden circle framework to explain why some companies and leaders are more successful than others. His powerful message about starting with "why" instead of "what" or "how" resonated with millions, making his presentation a classic example of persuasive communication.

5. <u>Airbnb's Rebranding Pitch by Airbnb's CEO Brian Chesky:</u>

When Airbnb underwent a rebranding, CEO Brian Chesky presented the new brand identity to the world. The presentation was bold and visually stunning, and Chesky explained the rationale behind the change, the company's vision, and the impact they aimed to create. The presentation showcased the power of storytelling and visuals to convey a brand's essence effectively.

6. <u>The "I Have a Dream" Speech by Martin Luther King Jr.:</u>

While not a traditional business presentation, Martin Luther King Jr.'s "I Have a Dream" speech is a prime example of a compelling and powerful pitch. Delivered during the March on Washington for Jobs and Freedom in 1963, this historic speech advocated for civil rights and equality. King's eloquence, passion, and vision for a better future moved the audience and left an enduring impact on the Civil Rights Movement.

7. <u>Pepsi's "Pepsi Challenge" Marketing Pitch:</u>

In the 1970s, Pepsi launched the "Pepsi Challenge," a blind taste test campaign challenging consumers to compare Pepsi to its main competitor, Coca-Cola. The company conducted live taste tests across the country, and the results were shared in commercials and presentations. The campaign's success highlighted the power of effective market research and the impact of engaging the audience directly in the marketing process.

These examples showcase the power of compelling storytelling, clear communication, and engaging visuals in successful presentations and pitches. Whether in business, education, or social movements, these influential presentations have left a lasting impression on their audiences and achieved their intended objectives.

Identify and Understand Your Target Market

Identify the ideal target market and conduct effective market research.

Identifying the ideal target market and conducting effective market research are vital steps for Rainmakers looking to achieve success in their business endeavors. Before diving into market research, it's crucial to have a clear understanding of your value proposition. Knowing what makes your product or service unique and how it addresses your customers' needs will guide you in finding the right audience.

Understanding your current customer base is a valuable starting point. Analyzing the characteristics, demographics, and behaviors of your existing customers can provide insights into who is already attracted to your offering. This information can be instrumental in identifying similar prospects in the market and crafting targeted marketing strategies.

To gain deeper insights into your target market, engage in surveys and interviews with both current customers and potential prospects. By actively listening to their feedback and understanding their pain points, preferences, and motivations, you can refine your marketing approach and tailor your offerings to meet their needs more effectively.

Monitoring social media platforms and online forums is another powerful tool for market research. Social media listening allows you to tap into conversations about your industry, brand, or competitors. By observing discussions and feedback, you can gain a better understanding of customer sentiments and identify potential gaps in the market.

Analyzing your competitors is an essential part of market research. Understanding how other players in your industry position themselves, target their markets, and differentiate their offerings can help you identify opportunities and areas for improvement in your own business strategy.

Market segmentation is a valuable technique for categorizing your target market into specific groups based on characteristics such as demographics, behavior, geography, or psychographics. This approach allows you to tailor your marketing efforts to effectively reach and engage each segment.

Creating detailed buyer personas is a powerful way to humanize your target audience. These fictional characters represent your ideal customers, going beyond demographics to understand their motivations, goals, challenges, and preferred communication channels. Buyer personas help align your messaging and strategies to better resonate with your customers.

Leveraging industry reports and data provides a broader view of the market landscape and trends. Market research reports can offer valuable insights into the overall market size, growth potential, and key competitors. Staying informed about your industry can help you identify opportunities and stay competitive.

Before fully committing to a specific target market or marketing strategy, conduct small-scale tests and pilot campaigns. Measuring the outcomes and using the results to validate assumptions and refine your approach will lead to more effective marketing efforts.

Lastly, it's essential to recognize that market research is not a one-time activity. Customer needs, preferences, and market dynamics change over time. Continuously monitor and adapt your strategies based on new information and insights to stay relevant and better serve your target market.

By investing in market research and understanding their target audience, Rainmakers can refine their business strategies, make informed decisions, and create meaningful connections with their customers, leading to long-term success and growth.

Explain how to customize the sales approach to fit the specific needs of the target market.

Customizing the sales approach to fit the specific needs of the target market is essential for Rainmakers to effectively engage potential customers and increase their chances of success. It begins with conducting thorough research and analysis of the target market, gaining a deep understanding of their demographics, preferences, pain points, and buying behavior. This information serves as the foundation for tailoring the sales approach.

One effective strategy is to develop detailed buyer personas that represent different segments of the target market. Each persona outlines the specific needs, challenges, goals, and preferences of the customers within that segment. With this segmentation in place, the sales approach can be customized to cater to the unique needs of each group.

Crafting sales messaging is a crucial aspect of customization. The language and examples used should resonate with the specific industry or profession of each segment, demonstrating a deep understanding of their unique challenges. Highlighting the benefits and solutions most relevant to each segment is essential to showcase how the product or service addresses their specific needs and provides value.

Utilizing social proof, such as customer reviews and testimonials, can build credibility and trust with the target market. Positive feedback from customers within the same industry can influence the buying decisions of potential customers.

Adaptability is vital when it comes to sales pitches. Each segment may respond differently to different approaches. Some may prefer formal presentations, while others might respond better to a casual and conversational style. Identifying the preferred communication channels of the target market and using them effectively is crucial to reach potential customers.

Offering customized pricing and packages is another way to cater to the specific needs and budgets of each segment, making the offering more appealing and accessible. Providing ongoing personalized support and assistance after making a sale can contribute to a positive post-sale experience.

Continuously seeking feedback from customers within each target market and using their insights to refine and improve the sales approach ensures that it remains relevant and effective over time.

By personalizing the sales approach to fit the specific needs of the target market, Rainmakers can establish stronger connections with potential customers, increase their chances of closing deals, and build a reputation as a reliable and customer-centric business. Understanding the unique requirements of each segment and tailoring the messaging and solutions accordingly will significantly contribute to sales success and long-term growth.

Focus on Building Relationships

Illustrate the importance of creating authentic relationships with clients.

Creating authentic relationships with clients is paramount for Rainmakers and any business seeking sustained success and growth. Authentic relationships go beyond merely transacting business; they are built on trust, transparency, and genuine care for the client's well-being.

The foundation of these relationships is trust. When clients feel that they are dealing with a genuine and honest individual or organization, they are more likely to trust your advice, recommendations, and offerings. Trust, in turn, leads to client loyalty, as they choose to continue working with someone they know has their best interests at heart.

Authentic relationships are the bedrock of long-term partnerships. When clients feel valued and understood, they are more likely to engage in repeat business and consider you as a preferred partner for future projects or needs. Long-term partnerships offer stability and a continuous revenue stream for the business.

Satisfied clients who have experienced authentic interactions are more likely to refer others to your business through word-of-mouth. Positive word-of-mouth marketing can significantly impact your reputation and attract new clients, often at a lower customer acquisition cost compared to other marketing efforts.

An authentic relationship encourages open and honest communication. Clients feel comfortable sharing their true needs, pain points, and expectations. This understanding allows Rainmakers to tailor their products or services to precisely meet those needs, leading to higher customer satisfaction.

In any business relationship, challenges are bound to arise. An authentic relationship fosters open communication, making it easier to address issues and find solutions together. Clients are more likely to work collaboratively in finding resolutions, leading to better outcomes and stronger partnerships.

As client needs evolve over time, an authentic relationship enables Rainmakers to adapt and pivot their offerings accordingly. By understanding the evolving requirements of their clients, businesses can stay relevant and provide continued value.

Authentic relationships contribute to higher customer lifetime value. Loyal and satisfied clients are more likely to engage in repeat business, upgrade to higher-value products or services, and invest in additional offerings from the same provider.

Creating authentic relationships with clients goes beyond transactions; it creates emotional connections between clients and the business. Clients become advocates for the brand, promoting it not just for its offerings but also for the positive experience they've had with the company.

Fostering authentic relationships with clients often goes hand in hand with promoting a positive organizational culture within the business. An emphasis on authenticity and client-centric values permeates throughout the organization, impacting how employees interact with clients and each other.

In conclusion, creating authentic relationships with clients is not just about achieving short-term gains; it's about building the foundation for lasting partnerships, trust, and mutual success. Authenticity builds bridges of understanding, enhances the customer experience, and sets the stage for continued growth and prosperity in business.

Tips on building trust and providing exceptional customer service.

Building trust and providing exceptional customer service are two crucial pillars for Rainmakers in establishing long-lasting and successful business relationships. Transparency and honesty form the bedrock of trust-building. When you communicate openly with your customers, being candid about your products, services, pricing, and any limitations, you foster an environment of trust. By avoiding unrealistic promises and consistently delivering on your commitments, customers will perceive your reliability and authenticity.

Active listening is another fundamental aspect of providing exceptional customer service. Taking the time to genuinely understand your customers' needs, concerns, and feedback demonstrates that you value their input. Show empathy and understanding during interactions, and respond promptly and courteously to their inquiries or issues. Timely responses exhibit respect for their time and further build trust in your commitment to serving their needs.

To create exceptional customer experiences, aim to exceed expectations whenever possible. By going the extra mile and providing personalized service or unexpected perks, you leave a lasting positive impression. This proactive approach not only increases customer satisfaction but also fosters loyalty and word-of-mouth referrals, leading to business growth.

Investing in training your employees and empowering them to make decisions that benefit customers is vital for consistent and exceptional customer service. Well-trained and empowered staff can handle customer inquiries and issues efficiently, resolving problems promptly and effectively.

Resolving complaints gracefully is a crucial skill in customer service. When customers express dissatisfaction or concerns, address their complaints with sincerity and a genuine willingness to find a resolution. Apologize when appropriate and offer viable solutions to show your commitment to rectifying the situation.

Personalizing interactions is an effective way to make customers feel valued and understood as individuals. Addressing customers by name and using their purchase history or preferences to tailor interactions creates a sense of rapport and fosters stronger customer relationships.

Consistency across all customer service channels is essential to maintain your brand's reputation and customer satisfaction. Regardless of whether customers interact with your business in person, on the phone, or online, ensuring they receive the same level of service reflects your commitment to delivering a positive experience.

Actively seeking customer feedback is an invaluable practice. Regularly gathering feedback through surveys, follow-up calls, or feedback forms enables you to understand your customers' evolving needs and make continuous improvements to your products and services.

Show appreciation for customer loyalty by implementing loyalty programs, special discounts, or exclusive offers. Recognizing and rewarding loyal customers not only strengthens the bond but also encourages repeat business and advocacy.

Anticipating customer needs and proactively offering solutions demonstrate a customer-centric approach. By addressing potential issues before customers even raise them, you demonstrate foresight and a commitment to ensuring their success.

Having a comprehensive knowledge base about your products or services equips your team to address customer queries accurately and confidently. A well-informed team can provide more personalized and effective solutions, enhancing the overall customer experience.

Remaining calm and professional in difficult situations is critical. Handling upset customers with composure and working towards finding a resolution without becoming defensive reinforces your commitment to exceptional customer service.

Celebrating your customers' successes and milestones shows genuine interest in their growth and accomplishments. Acknowledging their achievements fosters a positive emotional connection and reinforces the relationship.

By diligently implementing these strategies, Rainmakers can build trust with customers and provide exceptional customer service. Cultivating loyal and satisfied customers will result in positive word-of-mouth, repeat business, and a reputation for excellence, contributing to long-term success and growth.

Set Clear Goals

Setting measurable and achievable sales goals.

Setting measurable and achievable sales goals is a critical aspect of a Rainmaker's success. These goals serve as a roadmap, guiding them towards the growth and prosperity of their business. To effectively set these goals, a systematic and well-defined approach is necessary.

First and foremost, it is essential to define specific and clear sales objectives. These objectives could include increasing revenue, acquiring new customers, boosting repeat sales, or expanding into new markets. Having a precise understanding of what you want to achieve will help you stay focused and aligned with your business vision.

One effective framework for setting sales goals is the SMART criteria: Specific, Measurable, Achievable, Relevant, and Time-bound. This framework ensures that your goals are well-defined and realistic. It encourages you to set targets that can be quantified and measured, making it easier to track progress and evaluate success.

When determining measurable targets, consider your historical sales data and industry benchmarks. Analyzing past sales performance can provide valuable insights into your average sales growth and identify areas for improvement. Benchmarking against industry standards allows you to set achievable goals that are in line with the performance of your peers.

For long-term sales goals, it is beneficial to break them down into smaller, more manageable milestones. These milestones act as stepping stones towards your ultimate goal and allow you to track progress more frequently. Breaking down large goals into smaller targets also prevents them from becoming overwhelming and helps maintain motivation.

To ensure the goals are practical and achievable, involve your sales team in the goal-setting process. Their on-the-ground insights and feedback are invaluable in setting realistic targets that align with their capabilities and challenges. When your team feels invested in the goals, they are more likely to be motivated to achieve them.

Setting deadlines for each goal is crucial for creating a sense of urgency and accountability. Specific time frames provide a clear sense of direction and help prioritize tasks. Deadlines also serve as benchmarks for evaluating progress and determining if adjustments are necessary.

Regularly monitor your sales team's progress towards the goals. This involves closely reviewing performance metrics, conducting regular check-ins, and holding team meetings to discuss progress and identify areas that need improvement. Consistent monitoring helps in identifying any roadblocks early on and enables you to take corrective actions promptly.

In addition to setting goals, providing your sales team with the necessary resources, training, and support is vital. Adequate support ensures that your team has the tools and knowledge they need to achieve their targets effectively.

Recognize and celebrate milestones and successes along the way. Positive reinforcement and celebration boost team morale and motivation. Acknowledging achievements also reinforces the idea that the team's efforts are valued and appreciated.

Be open to adjusting goals if circumstances change or new opportunities arise. Being flexible in your approach allows you to adapt to market dynamics and stay responsive to changing customer needs.

Finally, analyze the results and performance at the end of each period. Identify what worked well and what could be improved. Use these insights to refine your approach for future goal-setting, continuously seeking growth and improvement.

By adopting this systematic approach to setting measurable and achievable sales goals, Rainmakers can inspire their sales team, track progress effectively, and propel their business towards sustained success. These goals serve as a roadmap for growth, guiding them towards their vision and ensuring that they remain competitive in their market.

How to monitor progress and adapt strategies if needed.

Monitoring progress and adapting strategies are essential components of successful sales management for Rainmakers. To effectively monitor progress and make necessary adjustments, several key steps should be followed.

Firstly, it is crucial to define key performance indicators (KPIs) that align with your sales goals. These KPIs could include metrics like revenue, number of new customers acquired, conversion rates, average order value, or customer retention rate. By having clear KPIs in place, you can measure and track your team's performance more effectively.

Utilizing sales tracking tools and software is another important step in monitoring progress. These tools provide real-time insights into your team's performance, customer behavior, and market trends. With access to up-to-date data, you can make informed decisions and identify areas that require improvement.

Setting regular review periods is essential for assessing progress towards your sales goals. Depending on the scale and complexity of your business, these reviews can be conducted monthly, quarterly, or semi-annually. During these review periods, you should analyze the performance data captured by your sales tracking tools. Evaluate how your team is performing against the set KPIs and identify any areas where they are excelling or falling short.

Recognizing and celebrating successes achieved by your sales team is crucial for boosting morale and motivation. Positive reinforcement can inspire your team to continue performing well. Additionally, it is essential to identify any challenges or roadblocks hindering progress. Understanding the obstacles your team faces allows you to address them and develop strategies for improvement.

Involving your sales team in the review process is vital. Seek their feedback and insights on what strategies are working well and what improvements they suggest. Their firsthand experience on the field can provide valuable information and foster a collaborative approach to finding solutions.

Customer feedback is an invaluable source of information for understanding their experience with your products or services. Analyze customer feedback to identify areas of improvement or opportunities for growth. Staying informed about market trends, changes in customer behavior, and competitor activities is also essential. This information helps you understand how external factors may impact your sales strategies and enables you to stay ahead of the competition.

If you're implementing new sales strategies or marketing campaigns, consider conducting A/B testing. This involves testing different approaches with different segments of your audience to identify which one yields better results. The insights gained from A/B testing can inform your decision-making process and lead to more effective strategies.

Based on the insights gathered from data analysis, customer feedback, and team input, make adjustments to your sales strategies and goals as necessary. Be open to making changes to ensure your approach remains relevant and effective in a dynamic business environment.

Providing ongoing training and support to your sales team is crucial, especially when adapting strategies. Equipping them with the necessary skills and knowledge ensures they can execute the revised strategies effectively and stay motivated to achieve the adjusted goals.

Clear communication is key when implementing changes. Communicate any adjustments to your sales strategies and goals to the entire team, explaining the rationale behind these changes. This ensures that everyone understands the reasons for the shift and can fully commit to the new direction.

By closely monitoring progress, analyzing data, and seeking feedback, Rainmakers can gain valuable insights into the effectiveness of their sales strategies. This data-driven approach allows them to adapt their tactics and make informed decisions to achieve their sales goals effectively. Regular review and adjustment are essential to staying competitive, responsive to market changes, and continuously improving sales performance.

Be Persistent and Resilient

Overcoming challenges and handle rejection constructively.

Persistence and resilience are essential qualities for Rainmakers to navigate the challenges of the sales profession successfully. In the dynamic and competitive world of sales, setbacks and rejections are inevitable. However, with persistence and resilience, Rainmakers can overcome these challenges and handle rejection constructively.

To begin with, maintaining a growth mindset is fundamental to persistence and resilience. Rather than viewing challenges and rejections as failures, see them as opportunities to learn and grow. A growth mindset empowers you to adapt, improve, and persevere through difficult situations.

In the sales field, it is crucial to set realistic expectations. Understand that not every prospect will convert into a customer immediately. Set achievable goals, and recognize that success in sales often comes through consistent effort and dedication. Stay committed to the process and be patient with yourself.

Resilience is the ability to bounce back from setbacks and disappointments. Cultivate resilience by focusing on the positives, seeking solutions to challenges, and not dwelling on the negatives. Develop the capacity to learn from rejections. Instead of taking rejection personally, view it as an opportunity to improve. Analyze the reasons for the rejection, seek feedback from prospects if possible, and use the insights gained to refine your approach.

Building a support network can provide encouragement during challenging times. Connect with mentors, colleagues, or sales coaches who can offer guidance and feedback to help you navigate difficulties effectively. Celebrate the small victories along the way. Recognizing progress, no matter how incremental, can boost morale and keep you motivated.

In the fast-paced sales environment, adaptability is crucial. Be open to trying new strategies, embracing change, and adjusting your approach based on feedback and market trends. Maintain a focus on finding solutions when facing challenges. Approach obstacles with a problem-solving mindset, and be proactive in seeking ways to overcome them.

Taking care of yourself is vital for maintaining resilience. Prioritize self-care by getting enough rest, exercising regularly, and engaging in activities that recharge and rejuvenate you. A positive attitude can be a powerful tool in overcoming challenges and handling rejection constructively. Focus on what you can control and maintain optimism in the face of setbacks.

Invest in continuous learning and professional development. The more you improve your skills and knowledge, the better equipped you will be to handle challenges and achieve sales success. Embracing persistence and resilience, Rainmakers can navigate the ups and downs of the sales journey with confidence. Overcoming challenges and handling rejection constructively are essential skills that will not only lead to sales success but also personal and professional growth. Remember that setbacks are temporary, and with determination and a positive mindset, you can turn challenges into opportunities for growth and achievement.

Strategies for maintaining motivation and determination in pursuing success.

Maintaining motivation and determination is crucial for Rainmakers to pursue success in their endeavors. The sales profession can be challenging and demanding, making it essential to employ strategies that keep them driven and focused on their goals.

One effective strategy is to set clear and meaningful goals. Having well-defined objectives provides a sense of purpose and direction. Rainmakers should define specific and achievable goals that align with their long-term vision. Breaking down these goals into smaller milestones allows them to celebrate progress along the way, boosting their motivation.

Visualization is a powerful technique to maintain motivation. Envisioning oneself achieving the goals and experiencing success can fuel determination. By embracing a positive mindset and believing in their capabilities to overcome obstacles, Rainmakers can stay focused on their journey to success.

Cultivating a growth mindset is another essential aspect. Adopting a growth mindset involves embracing challenges as opportunities for learning and improvement. Rainmakers can view failures as stepping stones to success rather than setbacks. This mindset encourages continuous development and resilience, enabling them to persevere through difficulties.

Surrounding oneself with positive influences is crucial for maintaining motivation. Having a supportive network of colleagues, mentors, or motivational materials can uplift and inspire Rainmakers to stay motivated on their journey. Engaging in discussions and activities that foster positivity can reinforce their determination.

Celebrating even the smallest achievements is important. By acknowledging and celebrating progress, Rainmakers can boost their motivation. Recognizing their efforts and giving themselves credit for the hard work invested in pursuing their goals keeps them motivated.

Maintaining a structured approach to work is beneficial. Staying organized and prioritizing tasks help Rainmakers avoid feeling overwhelmed. A clear focus on essential activities allows them to stay on track and avoid distractions, which is crucial for maintaining determination.

Taking regular breaks and practicing self-care is essential for avoiding burnout. By recharging and engaging in activities that bring joy and relaxation, Rainmakers can reinvigorate their motivation. A refreshed mind and body can keep them determined during challenging times.

Rainmakers should seek opportunities for continuous learning. Embracing a thirst for knowledge, attending workshops, reading books, and participating in training programs can enhance their skills and knowledge. Continuous learning fosters growth and keeps motivation high. Finding purpose in their work is important for Rainmakers. Understanding the impact of their work and connecting with the value they bring to customers can fuel determination. A sense of purpose empowers them to stay motivated during challenging times.

Establishing milestones on their journey to success and rewarding themselves upon achieving them is a helpful practice. Celebrating with small rewards, like treating oneself to something enjoyable or taking time off, reinforces the sense of accomplishment and maintains motivation.

Creating a positive work environment is crucial. Surrounding themselves with colleagues who share their drive for success and encourage each other's growth can foster motivation and determination.

Regularly reviewing progress towards their goals is essential. Rainmakers should assess what's working well and identify areas that need improvement. By adjusting their strategies based on these reviews, they can stay on course and maintain their determination.

By implementing these strategies, Rainmakers can maintain high levels of motivation and determination in their pursuit of success. These practices foster a positive and resilient mindset, ensuring they stay focused and driven in the face of challenges. A steadfast commitment to their goals empowers them to overcome obstacles and achieve the level of success they desire.

Continuously Learn and Improve

Invest in the personal and professional development.

Investing in your personal and professional development is one of the most rewarding decisions you can make in your life. It is a journey of growth, learning, and self-discovery that can lead to incredible opportunities and fulfillment. By dedicating time and resources to develop yourself, you open the door to endless possibilities and unlock your true potential.

Remember, personal and professional development is not just about acquiring new skills and knowledge, but also about cultivating a growth mindset. Embrace the idea that you can always improve and evolve, no matter your age or current level of expertise. This mindset empowers you to face challenges with confidence and adapt to the ever-changing world around you.

Investing in your personal development means taking the time to understand yourself better. Discover your passions, strengths, and areas for improvement. By gaining self-awareness, you can make more informed decisions about your career path and life goals, leading to a more fulfilling and purpose-driven life.

On the professional front, continuous development is crucial for staying competitive in the modern workforce. The world is evolving rapidly, and new technologies and trends emerge constantly. By investing in your professional skills and knowledge, you position yourself as a valuable asset to employers and clients alike.

Furthermore, personal and professional development goes hand in hand. As you grow personally, your professional life will also see positive impacts. Improved communication skills, enhanced emotional intelligence, and increased self-confidence are just a few of the benefits that spill over into your career.

Investing in yourself sends a powerful message that you value your growth and potential. It shows that you are committed to lifelong learning and dedicated to reaching new heights. Others will recognize and appreciate your willingness to invest in yourself, making you stand out in both personal and professional circles.

Remember that investing in personal and professional development is not a one-time event. It is a continuous journey of improvement and learning. Embrace every opportunity to learn, whether through formal education, workshops, networking events, or even self-guided learning. Seek feedback from mentors and peers to gain valuable insights into your progress and areas of improvement.

As you invest in yourself, you'll find that the rewards are immeasurable. Your newfound skills, confidence, and growth will lead you to exciting opportunities and open doors that you may never have thought possible. Embrace this journey of self-discovery and development, and watch as it transforms your life in ways you could have never imagined. Your future self will thank you for making the investment in your personal and professional development today. So, take that leap, and let your potential soar!

A short list of resources to continue learning and staying updated on industry trends.

1. **Online Courses and Platforms**: Websites like Coursera, Udemy, LinkedIn Learning, and Skillshare offer a wide range of online courses on various topics, including sales, marketing, leadership, and industry-specific subjects.

2 . **Industry Publications and Magazines**: Subscribe to industry-specific publications and magazines to stay updated on the latest trends, news, and insights in your field.

3. **Professional Associations**: Join relevant professional associations or organizations in your industry. These associations often offer webinars, workshops, and conferences to keep members informed about industry developments.

4 . **Podcasts**: Listen to industry-related podcasts hosted by experts

and thought leaders. Podcasts are a convenient way to learn during commutes or downtime.

5 . **Webinars and Virtual Events**: Attend webinars and virtual events hosted by industry experts or companies. These events provide valuable insights and networking opportunities.

6. **Blogs and Websites**: Follow influential blogs and websites related to your industry. They often provide in-depth articles, case studies, and analysis of current trends.

7. **Social Media**: Follow industry thought leaders, influencers, and companies on social media platforms like LinkedIn, Twitter, and Instagram. They often share valuable content and insights.

8. **Books and E-books**: Read books and e-books written by experts in your industry. They offer comprehensive knowledge and actionable strategies.

9 . **Industry Forums and Online Communities**: Participate in industry forums and online communities to engage with peers, ask questions, and share knowledge.

10. **Research Papers and Whitepapers**: Access research papers and whitepapers published by reputable organizations and institutions. They provide data-driven insights into industry trends.

11. **YouTube Channels**: Subscribe to YouTube channels that focus on your industry or relevant topics. Many channels offer educational videos and tutorials.

1 2 . **Industry Conferences and Seminars**: Attend industry conferences and seminars (in-person or virtual) to learn from keynote speakers, panel discussions, and networking opportunities.

13. **Mentors and Networking**: Connect with mentors and industry professionals who can provide guidance and share their experiences.

14. **Google Alerts**: Set up Google Alerts for relevant keywords to

receive email notifications on the latest news and articles related to your industry.

15. **News Aggregator Apps**: Use news aggregator apps to curate and deliver industry-specific news and updates directly to your mobile device.

Remember to stay proactive in seeking out these resources regularly. Continuous learning is a key aspect of personal and professional growth, and leveraging these resources will help you stay ahead in your industry and remain competitive in the ever-changing business landscape.

Provide Exceptional Customer Service

Customer satisfaction can lead to new sales opportunities.

Customer satisfaction is a powerful catalyst for generating new sales opportunities in a business. When customers are genuinely satisfied with a product or service they have received, they are more likely to become loyal advocates and promoters of the brand. Satisfied customers often share their positive experiences with friends, family, and colleagues through word-of-mouth referrals, social media, or online reviews. These recommendations carry significant weight, as potential buyers tend to trust the opinions of existing customers more than traditional advertising.

Furthermore, customer satisfaction enhances brand reputation and credibility. A business that consistently delivers on its promises and exceeds customer expectations establishes a positive reputation in the market. This reputation not only attracts new customers but also draws the attention of potential business partners, investors, and collaborators. Satisfied customers are more inclined to provide testimonials and case studies, which can be utilized in marketing efforts to showcase the real-world impact of the product or service.

Additionally, customer satisfaction drives repeat business and fosters long-term relationships. A satisfied customer is more likely to return for future purchases, leading to increased customer lifetime value. These repeat customers often spend more over time and become a stable source of revenue for the business. Moreover, satisfied customers are more receptive to upselling or cross-selling opportunities, allowing the business to expand its offerings to meet their evolving needs.

In the digital age, customer satisfaction plays a pivotal role in online visibility and search engine rankings. Positive customer feedback and reviews influence search algorithms, boosting the business's online visibility and organic traffic. This increased visibility attracts a broader audience and exposes the brand to potential customers who might not have discovered it otherwise.

Furthermore, satisfied customers tend to provide valuable feedback and insights that can lead to product or service improvements. By listening to their customers, businesses can identify pain points, address issues, and implement changes that enhance the overall customer experience. This continuous improvement process not only strengthens customer loyalty but also makes the product or service more appealing to potential buyers.

Customer satisfaction is a key driver of new sales opportunities. Satisfied customers act as brand ambassadors, attracting new buyers through positive word-of-mouth and referrals. A strong reputation based on customer satisfaction opens doors to partnerships, collaborations, and investor interest. The loyalty of satisfied customers drives repeat business and upselling opportunities, maximizing customer lifetime value. Additionally, customer feedback contributes to product enhancements, ensuring the brand remains competitive and appealing to potential customers. By prioritizing customer satisfaction, businesses can unlock a wealth of new sales opportunities and foster sustainable growth in the market.

Tips for providing outstanding customer service and exceeding customer expectations.

Providing outstanding customer service and exceeding customer expectations is key to building strong customer loyalty and growing a successful business. Here are some valuable tips to achieve this:

Active Listening: Listen carefully to your customers' needs and concerns. Pay attention to their feedback, whether positive or negative, and use it to improve your products or services.

Personalization: Treat each customer as an individual and personalize your interactions. Address them by their name, remember their preferences, and tailor your solutions to their specific needs.

Prompt Responses: Respond to customer inquiries and issues promptly. Aim to resolve problems in a timely manner to demonstrate your commitment to their satisfaction.

Anticipate Needs: Proactively anticipate your customers' needs and offer solutions before they even ask. Providing proactive assistance shows that you truly care about their experience.

Empathy and Understanding: Show empathy and understanding towards your customers' situations. Put yourself in their shoes to better relate to their concerns and emotions.

Go the Extra Mile: Always be willing to go above and beyond to exceed customer expectations. Surprise them with unexpected gestures of goodwill, such as discounts, freebies, or personalized thank-you notes.

Consistency: Ensure that every interaction with your business, whether in-person, online, or over the phone, reflects the same high level of customer service. Consistency builds trust and reliability.

Respect Customer's Time: Value your customers' time by providing quick and efficient service. Minimize wait times and offer self-service options when appropriate.

Ask for Feedback: Regularly seek feedback from your customers through surveys or feedback forms. Use this information to identify areas for improvement and to gauge customer satisfaction.

Handle Complaints with Grace: When faced with complaints, remain calm and courteous. Address the issue promptly and professionally, aiming to turn a negative experience into a positive one.

Keep Promises: Never overpromise and underdeliver. Be honest and realistic about what you can offer, and then deliver on those promises consistently.

Celebrate Success Stories: Share success stories and testimonials from happy customers. This can build trust and credibility among potential customers.

Continuous Improvement: Regularly review and improve your customer service processes. Keep learning and adapting to meet changing customer expectations.

Express Gratitude: Show genuine gratitude to your customers for choosing your business. A simple "thank you" can go a long way in making customers feel valued.

By applying these tips consistently, you can create a customer-centric culture that delights your customers and sets your business apart from competitors. Exceptional customer service not only leads to customer loyalty but also generates positive word-of-mouth and referrals, driving further growth and success for your business.

Conclusion

As we have seen throughout the book, the journey to becoming a true Rainmaker involves mastering a set of essential skills and adopting specific attributes. A Rainmaker is characterized by **persistence, resilience, adaptability, and a growth mindset**. These qualities are crucial for navigating the challenges of the sales profession and turning setbacks into opportunities for growth and improvement.

As we have learned, expert **knowledge of the product or service** being offered is vital. Understanding the features and benefits of what one is selling enables Rainmakers to effectively communicate value to potential clients. This knowledge empowers Rainmakers to connect with customers on a deeper level and build trust, a foundation for **long-lasting relationships**.

Building and nurturing professional relationships are emphasized as a central aspect of Rainmaking. Networking and expanding one's circle of contacts are essential steps for Rainmakers to reach new clients and open doors to potential opportunities. The book highlights the significance of **authenticity** in these relationships, as genuine connections lead to more meaningful partnerships.

The importance of setting measurable and achievable sales goals cannot be overstated. Regularly monitoring progress and adapting strategies based on data-driven insights help Rainmakers stay on track and make necessary adjustments to achieve success.

As we delve into the importance of customer satisfaction, the book emphasizes how happy customers can become valuable brand advocates. Satisfied clients are more likely to share positive experiences with others, generating new sales opportunities through word-of-mouth **referrals and testimonials**.

Moreover, **investing in personal and professional development** is a recurring theme in the book. Continuously improving skills and knowledge ensures Rainmakers stay ahead in a competitive market, providing an edge that distinguishes them from others in the field.

In conclusion, the book paints a comprehensive picture of the attributes and practices that define real successful Rainmakers. By embracing the lessons learned and putting the valuable insights into practice, readers can embark on a transformative journey to becoming true Rainmakers. With determination, dedication, and a commitment to personal growth, readers have the opportunity to excel in the sales profession, creating a lasting impact on their businesses and achieving remarkable success as Rainmakers. Embrace the Rainmaker mentality and embark on this transformative path to flourish as a sales professional.

www.ingramcontent.com/pod-product-compliance
Lightning Source LLC
Chambersburg PA
CBHW060007300526
45794CB00003B/1119

* 9 7 9 8 8 5 3 5 0 2 7 3 4 *